# THIS BOOK BELONGS TO A SPECIAL BEE NAMED

..............................................

..............................................

There was once a special bumblebee named Benny.
His dad was named Kenny and his mum was Penny!

Benny and his parents woke up bright and early
on an exciting day in the hive.
Benny buzzed with excitement, he felt so alive!
He said, "It's finally time, the flowers of spring are here!"
For bumblebees, this was surely the greatest day of the year.

He imagined the gardens he used to visit and the beautiful sight!
There were lilies, roses, daisies
and other flowers so colourful and bright.
"Well, i'm off to collect pollen and nectar for the colony!"
Benny said and headed on his way.
He flew out of the hive on that special spring day.

When Benny arrived at the flower field he used to visit,
he was full of surprise.
No longer were there flowers, but a factory of great big size!
A tired worker said, "Go away, get away bee!
Go buzz somewhere else and get away from me."

Benny said "Hmm, maybe they moved the flowers and planted them elsewhere."
Then he remembered another garden and sped right over there.

Benny was still happy about springtime
and he hummed a joyful song.
Then he arrived at the old garden, it didn't take very long.
"Huh? What's going on!?" he asked himself full of fear.
There was a neighbourhood of houses
that replaced the flowers that once lived here.

Benny felt someone swat his body, and boy did it hurt!
He landed right on a little boy's blue shirt.
"My son is allergic to creatures like you!
Why don't you go off and do what little bees do?"
An angry woman looked at him to say.
And Benny the bumblebee headed on his way.

Benny had not seen a single flower
so he started to worry.
And he rushed off to the last place he used to go
in a great big hurry.
He thought, "Surely this field of flowers
will be in full spring bloom!"
But Benny quickly learned,
that was the wrong thing to assume.

There were stores and restaurants
for as far as Benny could see,
And he thought, "Where are the precious flowers?
Oh, where could they be?"

A dog passed by Benny wearing a leash that was red,
"You are not welcome here!" the old dog said.
"Why don't you go look for some kind of tree."
"A flower. I am looking for a flower because I am a bee."

Benny buzzed away feeling oh so sad,
If he couldn't bring pollen to the colony, that would be very bad.
He said to himself, "Don't these humans know?
Without us pollinators, their food can't grow."

"Why build the buildings to take the marvellous nature away? There are no more flowers left," Benny was disappointed to say.

A little bee came over,
"Why hello, my name is Emma and i heard what you said,
But there are plenty of flowers and they are just up ahead!
There is a plant sanctuary with flowers
as marvellous as can be!
Come on, will you please follow me!"

Benny thought the whole flight, could it be true?
And then there it was, one magical view!
There was the greatest garden he had ever seen,
filled with working bees,
There were beautiful colours and fruit hanging from trees.

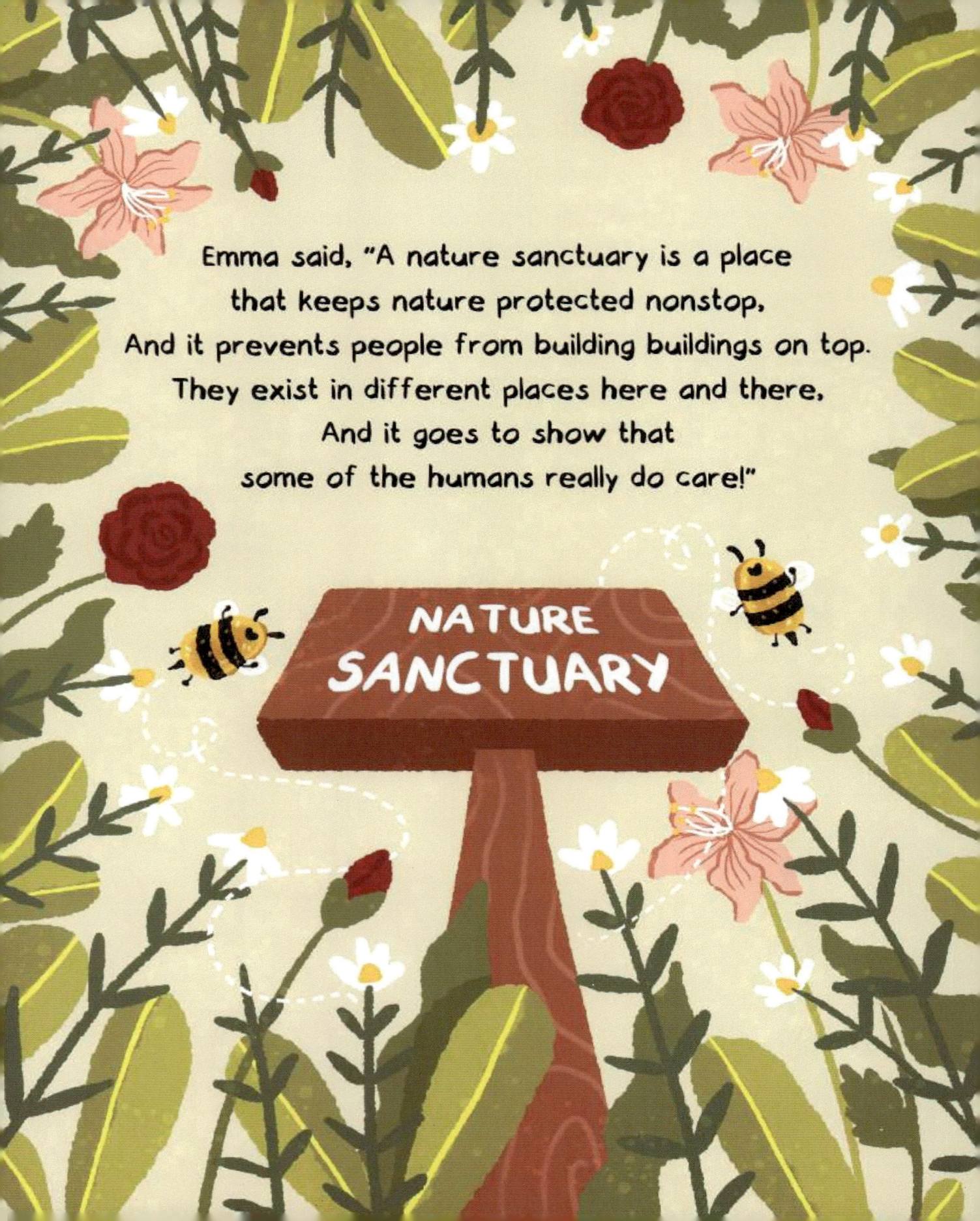

Emma said, "A nature sanctuary is a place
that keeps nature protected nonstop,
And it prevents people from building buildings on top.
They exist in different places here and there,
And it goes to show that
some of the humans really do care!"

NATURE SANCTUARY

Benny never felt happier, he had no words to say!
And he went on happily pollinating away.
When he brought pollen back home, the whole colony cheered!
And they were no longer worried
that all of the flowers disappeared.

Bees are like tiny superheroes,
but instead of capes they have wings,
And the pollinators change the world
with the pollinating powers that they bring.

"Hello, do you think you could help me and my friends?"

"Let me tell you a few things that make us Bee's happy."

PLANT A BEE FRIENDLY GARDEN.

FROM AS SMALL AS A SINGLE POT TO AS BIG AS YOU WISH, EVERY FLOWER HELPS.

ME AND MY FRIENDS GET ALOT OF OUR NECTAR FROM FLOWERING TREES. WHY NOT PLANT ONE TO HELP US BEE'S.

ON HOT DRY DAYS US BEE'S GET VERY THIRSTY!

WHY NOT MAKE A BEE DRINKING STATION TO HELP US.

Beekeepers work very hard to take care of us. So help us bees by buying local honey and supporting the beekeepers in your area. It tastes great too!

CHECK OUT YOUR LOCAL BEE CHARITIES FOR MORE WAYS TO HELP AND SUPPORT THE BEE FIGHT.

THANK YOU

SHOW OFF HOW YOU HELPED THE BEES BY USING THE HASHTAG #BENNYTHEBEE

BOOKSBYTHEBUTLER
#BENNYTHEBEE
TO FIND OUT MORE

Printed in Great Britain
by Amazon